TO

_____

FROM

_____

D0630373

A CHRISTMAS
TO REMEMBER

B
B

Brighton Books
Nashville, TN

A CHRISTMAS
TO REMEMBER

ISBN 1-58334-178-1

The quoted ideas expressed in this book (but not scripture verses) are not, in all cases, exact quotations, as some have been edited for clarity and brevity. In all cases, the author has attempted to maintain the speaker's original intent. In some cases, quoted material for this book was obtained from secondary sources, primarily print media. While every effort was made to ensure the accuracy of these sources, the accuracy cannot be guaranteed. For additions, deletions, corrections or clarifications in future editions of this text, please write Brighton Books.

Printed in the United States of America
Cover Design: Nick Long
Page Layout: Bart Dawson

1 2 3 4 5 6 7 8 9 10 • 02 03 04 05 06 07 08 09 10

For All Families Around the World

*A*mong our most precious earthly possessions are our memories, and few memories are more dear than those of Christmases past. But, it is important to consider that this year, like every year before it, is not only a time to revisit old memories; it is also a time to create new ones with our families and our friends. And, if we are to make meaningful memories, then this Christmas must begin and end with thanksgiving and praise for our Creator.

Are you caught up in the annual rush of the holiday season? If so, slow down long enough to consider the Bible verses and quotations that appear on the following pages. When you do, you'll be reminded that the best Christmas memories have little to do with material possessions. To the contrary, the moments that touch our hearts most profoundly are those times when we gather together with loved ones to share moments of fellowship and celebration.

This holiday can and should be a Christmas to remember. We will make it so if we share Christ's love and honor His Father.

TABLE OF CONTENTS

A CHILD IS BORN

For God so loved the world, that he gave his only begotten Son . . . .

John 3:16 KJV

he story of the first Christmas is told with beauty in the second chapter of Luke:

*And it came to pass in those days,
that there went out a decree from Caesar Augustus,
that all the world should be taxed….*

And all went to be taxed, every one into his own city. And Joseph also went up from Galilee, out of the city of Nazareth, into Judea, unto the city of David, which is called Bethlehem, (because he was of the house and lineage of David) to be taxed with Mary his espoused wife, being great with child. And so it was, that, while they were there, the days were accomplished that she should be delivered.

And she brought forth her firstborn son, and wrapped him in swaddling clothes, and laid him in a manger; because there was no room for them in the inn. And there were in the same country shepherds abiding in the field, keeping watch over their flock by night.

And, lo, the angel of the Lord came upon them, and the glory of the Lord shone round about them; and they were sore afraid. And the angel said unto them, Fear not: for, behold, I bring you good tidings of great joy, which shall be to all people. For unto you is born this day in the city of David a Saviour, which is Christ the Lord.

And this shall be a sign unto you; Ye shall find the babe
wrapped in swaddling clothes, lying in a manger. And suddenly
there was with the angel a multitude of the heavenly host
praising God, and saying, Glory to God
in the highest, and on earth peace,
good will toward men.

Luke 2:1-14 KJV

Infinite, and an infant. Eternal, and yet born of a woman.
Heir of all things, yet the carpenter's son.

C. H. Spurgeon

On Christmas Day two thousand years ago, the birth of a tiny baby
in an obscure village in the Middle East was
God's supreme triumph of good over evil.

Charles Colson

Christmas is about a baby, born in a stable,
who changed the world forever.

John Maxwell

The Son of God does not want to be seen
and found in heaven. Therefore
He descended from heaven to this earth
and came to us in our flesh.

Martin Luther

In this world you will have trouble.

But take heart!

I have overcome the world.

John 16:33 NIV

Jesus said . . .

If any man thirst, let him come unto me, and drink.

John 7:37 KJV

I am the door: by me if any man enter in, he shall be saved,
and shall go in and out, and find pasture.

John 10:9 KJV

I am the vine, ye are the branches.

John 15:5 KJV

Christ is no Moses, no exactor, no giver of laws, but a giver of grace,
a Savior; he is infinite mercy and goodness,
freely and bountifully given to us.

Martin Luther

In every Christian, Christ lives again. Every true believer
is a return to first-century Christianity.

Vance Havner

The Son of God became man to enable men to become sons of God.

C. S. Lewis

he old message "For unto you is born this day
in the city of David a Savior which is
Christ the Lord" is still the heart of Christmas.

Peter Marshall

29

Away in a Manger

Away in a manger, no crib for a bed,
The little Lord Jesus lay down his sweet head.
The stars in the sky looked down where he lay,
The little Lord Jesus, asleep on the hay.

The cattle are lowing, the baby awakes,
But little Lord Jesus, no crying he makes.
I love Thee, Lord Jesus! Look down from the sky,
And stand by my cradle till morning is nigh.

Anonymous

A Christmas Prayer

Dear Lord, during this Christmas season, keep me mindful of Your priceless gift: my personal Savior, Christ Jesus. Father, You loved me before I was ever born, and You will love me throughout eternity. In return, let me offer my life to You so that I might live according to Your commandments and according to Your plan. I give thanks for Your Son Jesus and for Your everlasting love.

Amen

A CHRISTMAS TO REMEMBER

I thank my God every time I remember you.

Philippians 1:3 NIV

Paul's letter to the Philippians was written from prison, yet the tone of the letter was joyful and triumphant. In addressing the Christians at Philippi, Paul observed that he thanked God every time he remembered his distant friends. And so it should be for us: when we think of distant friends and family members, we, too, should thank our Lord for our families, for our friends, and for our cherished memories.

We can make this Christmas a memorable one by sharing God's love and His message with all who cross our paths. When we do, we honor the Father and the One whose birth we celebrate.

Memories of hymns and carols keep the spirit of Christmas fresh.

Norman Vincent Peale

Happy, happy Christmas, that can win us back to the memories
of our childhood days, recall to the old man the pleasures
of his youth, and transport the traveler back to
his own fireside and quiet home!

Charles Dickens

Christmas, like God, is timeless and eternal.

Dale Evans

Every good and perfect gift is from above, coming down from
the Father of the heavenly lights,
who does not change like shifting shadows.

James 1:17 NIV

The heavens declare the glory of God; and the firmament
showeth his handiwork.

Psalm 19:1 KJV

O praise the LORD, all ye nations: praise him, all ye people.
For his merciful kindness is great toward us: and the truth
of the LORD endureth for ever. Praise ye the LORD.

Psalm 117:1-2 KJV

A Christmas Prayer

Thank you, Dear Lord, for memories of Christmases past.
Help me to make this Christmas a memorable celebration
of the birth of Your Son.

Amen

THE SPIRIT OF CHRISTMAS

I will put my Spirit in you and you will live . . . .

Ezekiel 37:14 NIV

*T*he Christmas Story begins in a faraway land: a babe is born, and the world is forever changed. And, if we are to celebrate Christmas as God intends, then we, too, must be forever changed.

Christ's message is a transforming message. May we carry that message to the world, not just on Christmas day, but on every day of the year. And may the Christmas spirit, which was born with a babe in Bethlehem, dwell forever in our hearts.

The Christmas message is delivered—the message
of the light of the world which breaks through
from above, always from above.

Karl Barth

For I am persuaded, that neither death, nor life,
nor angels, nor principalities, nor powers,
nor things present, nor things to come, nor height,
nor depth, nor any other creature, shall be able
to separate us from the love of God,
which is in Christ Jesus our Lord.

Romans 8:38-39 KJV

*C*hrist, the Son of God, the complete embodiment
of God's Word, came among us. He looked on
humanity's losing battle with sin and pitched
His divine tent in the middle of the camp
so that He could dwell among us.

Beth Moore

or the Son of man is come to save that which was lost.

Matthew 18:11 KJV

Take my yoke upon you, and learn of me;

for I am meek and lowly in heart:

and ye shall find rest unto your souls.

For my yoke is easy, and my burden is light.

Matthew 11:29-30 KJV

Has he taken over your heart? Perhaps he resides there,
but does he preside there?

Vance Havner

God wants to change our lives—and He will,
as we open our hearts to Him.

Billy Graham

Christ's work of making new men is not mere improvement,
but transformation.

C. S. Lewis

If we have the true love of God in our hearts,

we will show it in our lives.

We will not have to go up and down the earth proclaiming it.

We will show it in everything we say or do.

D. L. Moody

O little town of Bethlehem,
How still we see thee lie,
Above thy deep and dreamless sleep,
The silent stars go by;
Yet in thy dark streets shineth
The everlasting Light,
The hopes and fears of all the years
Are met in thee tonight.

O holy Child of Bethlehem!

Descend to us we pray;

Cast out our sin and enter in,

Be born in us today.

We hear the Christmas angels

The great glad tidings tell;

O come to us abide with us,

Our Lord Emmanuel!

Phillips Brooks, 1867

A Christmas Prayer

Lord, make me a joyful Christian, not just on Christmas day,
but every day of the year. Let me tell the story of Your Son,
not just at Christmastime, but during every season of the year.
Let me be Your generous, loving, faithful servant,
today, tomorrow, and forever.

Amen

A TIME FOR FAMILY AND FRIENDS

If we love one another, God dwelleth in us . . . .

1 John 4:12 KJV

At Christmastime, we gather together with family and friends to celebrate the joys of the season. And, when we share our holidays with those we love, we make memories that last a lifetime.

This Christmas, too, is an opportunity to make memories for ourselves, for our families, and for our friends. May those memories be as joyful as the season we celebrate.

A Christmas family-party!
We know of nothing in
nature more delightful!

Charles Dickens

No other structure can replace the family. Without it, our children
have no moral foundation. Without it, they become
moral illiterates whose only law is self.

Chuck Colson

It is a reverent thing to see an ancient castle or building not in decay,
or to see a fair timber tree sound and perfect.
How much more beautiful it is to behold an ancient and
noble family that has stood against the waves and weathers of time.

Francis Bacon

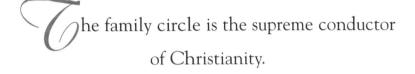

The family circle is the supreme conductor
of Christianity.

Henry Drummond

The best times in life are made a thousand times better
when shared with a dear friend.

Luci Swindoll

In friendship, God opens your eyes to the glories of Himself.

Joni Eareckson Tada

How good and pleasant it is when brothers live together in unity!

Psalm 133:1 NIV

A Christmas Prayer

*Dear Lord, I am blessed to be part of the family of God where
I find love and acceptance. You have also blessed me with my earthly
family. Today, Father, I give thanks for my family and for my friends.
May the love and acceptance that I give to them be a reflection
of the love and acceptance that You have shown for me.*

Amen

A SEASON FOR GIVING

God loves a cheerful giver.

2 Corinthians 9:7 NIV

he thread of generosity is woven completely and inextricably into the very fabric of Christ's teachings. If we are to be disciples of Christ, we, too, must give freely of our time, our love, and our possessions. During the Christmas season and throughout the year, we are called upon to be cheerful, generous, courageous givers. The world needs our help, but even more importantly, we need the spiritual rewards that God bestows upon us when we give cheerfully and without reservation.

Christmas day is a day of joy and charity.
May God make you very rich in both.

Phillips Brooks

Let us not become weary in doing good, for at the proper time
we will reap a harvest if we do not give up.

Galatians 6:9 NIV

And above all things have fervent charity among yourselves:
for charity shall cover the multitude of sins.

1 Peter 4:8 KJV

He that hath two coats, let him impart to him that hath none.

Luke 3:11 KJV

I tell you the truth, whatever you did for
one of the least of these brothers of mine,
you did for me.

Matthew 25:40 NIV

*S*omehow not only for Christmas

But all the long year through,

The joy that you give to others

Is the joy that comes back to you.

John Greenleaf Whittier

Let us give according to our incomes,
　　　　lest God make our incomes match our gifts.

Peter Marshall

We are never more like God than when we give.

Chuck Swindoll

Since you cannot do good to all, you are to pay special regard
　　　　to those who, by the accidents of time, or place,
　　or circumstances, are brought into closer connection with you.

Saint Augustine

*C*hristmas is most truly Christmas when we
celebrate it by giving the light of love
to those who need it most.

Ruth Carter Stapleton

*F*reely you have received, freely give.

Matthew 10:8 NIV

A Christmas Prayer

Lord, You have been so generous with me; let me be generous
with others. Help me to give generously of my time and
my possessions, not just during the Christmas season,
but throughout the year. And, make me a humble giver,
Lord, so that all the glory and the praise might be Yours.

Amen

A TIME FOR CELEBRATION

This is the day the LORD has made; let us rejoice and be glad in it.

Psalm 118:24 NIV

*T*he words on the previous page, taken from Psalm 118, remind us that today, like every other day, is a cause for celebration. God gives us this day; He fills it to the brim with possibilities, and He challenges us to use it for His purposes. The day is presented to us fresh and clean at midnight, free of charge, but we must beware: Today is a non-renewable resource—once it's gone, it's gone forever. Our utmost responsibility, of course, is to use this day in the service of God's will and according to His commandments.

On Christmas Day, we have special cause to celebrate: the birth of the Christ child. Let us praise God for His gift of His Son and the gift of this day. Both are priceless.

*M*erry Christmas to you!
May the glory that we celebrate
in this Christmas season fill your life
forever and ever.

Norman Vincent Peale

Have your heart right with Christ, and he will visit you often,
and so turn weekdays into Sundays, meals into sacraments,
homes into temples, and earth into heaven.

C. H. Spurgeon

To God be the glory; great things He hath done!
So loved He the world that He gave us His son.

Fanny Crosby

Jesus: the proof of God's love.

Philip Yancey

Let the hearts of those who seek the Lord rejoice.
Look to the Lord and his strength; seek his face always.

1 Chronicles 16:10-11 NIV

Rejoice evermore. Pray without ceasing. In every thing give thanks:
for this is the will of God in Christ Jesus concerning you.

1 Thessalonians 5:16-18 KJV

Rejoice, and be exceeding glad: for great is your reward in heaven....

Matthew 5:12 KJV

A Christmas Prayer

Dear Lord, You have given me so many reasons to celebrate.
During the Christmas season and throughout the year, let me choose
an attitude of cheerfulness. Let me be a joyful Christian, Lord,
quick to laugh and slow to anger. And, let me share Your goodness
with my family, my friends, and my neighbors,
this day and every day.

Amen

THROUGH THE EYES OF A CHILD

Suffer the little children to come unto me, and forbid them not;
for of such is the kingdom of God.

Mark 10:14 KJV

Christmas is a special time for children. As the big day nears, youngsters become more and more excited. And as adults, we can learn from their excitement. Materialism, of course, is a sign of spiritual immaturity, but joy is not. And while our children may look longingly at brightly wrapped gifts under the tree, we adults should fix our collective gaze much higher, at the star that symbolizes that night in Bethlehem when our Savior was born. Then, with childlike exuberance, we should encourage our children to enjoy the Christmas season while keeping them ever mindful that Christ is, and always will be, the greatest Christmas gift of all.

It is good to be children sometimes,
and never better than at Christmas,
when its mighty Founder was a child himself.

Charles Dickens

*W*hen Jesus put the little child in the midst of
His disciples, He did not tell the little child
to become like His disciples; He told the disciples
to become like the little child.

Ruth Bell Graham

*C*hildren are the hands by which
we take hold of heaven.

Henry Ward Beecher

Let us look upon our children; let us love them and train them
as children of the covenant and children of the promise.
These are the children of God.

Andrew Murray

A child is a beam of sunlight from the Infinite and Eternal.

Lyman Abbott

To love children is to love God.

Roy Rogers

81

A Christmas Prayer

Lord, the children of this world are Your children.
Let us love them, care for them, nurture them, teach them,
and lead them to You. And during this Christmas season,
as I serve as an example to the children under my care,
let my words and deeds demonstrate the love
that I feel for them . . . and for You.

Amen

A TIME FOR THANKSGIVING

Rejoice evermore. Pray without ceasing. In every thing give thanks:
for this is the will of God in Christ Jesus concerning you.

1 Thessalonians 5:16-18 KJV

Sometimes, in the crush of the holiday season, we simply don't stop long enough to pause and thank our Creator for the countless blessings He has bestowed upon us. But, when we neglect our God, we rob ourselves of the joy He intends for our lives. God has blessed us beyond measure, and we owe Him everything, including our praise. Let us praise Him always, and let us thank Him for the gift of His Son.

It is only with gratitude that life becomes rich.

Dietrich Bonhoeffer

A child of God should be a visible beatitude for happiness
and a living doxology for gratitude.

C. H. Spurgeon

Give thanks in all circumstances; for this is God's will
for you in Christ Jesus.

1 Thessalonians 5:18 NIV

Why wait until the fourth Thursday in November?
Thanksgiving to God should be an everyday affair.
The time to be thankful is now!

Jim Gallery

Thanks be to God for his indescribable gift!

2 Corinthians 9:15 NIV

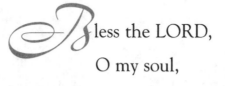

Bless the LORD,

O my soul,

and forget not all his benefits.

Psalm 103:2 KJV

Christmas is a good time to take stock of our blessings.

Pat Boone

The only real blind person at Christmastime is he who
has not Christmas in his heart.

Helen Keller

At Christmas, surroundings do not matter because the spirit of Jesus
is everywhere, knocking on the doors of our hearts.

Norman Vincent Peale

A Christmas Prayer

*Heavenly Father, Your gifts are greater than I can imagine.
May I live each day with thanksgiving in my heart and praise
on my lips. Thank You for the gift of Your Son and for the promise
of eternal life. During this season, let me share the joyous news
of Jesus' birth, and let my life be a testimony
to His love and to His grace.*

Amen

AND THE GREATEST OF THESE . . .

But now abide faith, hope, love, these three;
but the greatest of these is love.

1 Corinthians 13:13 NASB

*C*hristmas should be a time to celebrate, a time to contemplate, and a time to share feelings of warmth and appreciation with those we love. Let's make this holiday season a Christmas to remember by expressing our love and affection for family members and friends. When we do, we make ourselves dutiful servants of the One whose birth is the reason for this glorious season.

The greatest Christmas gift
is wrapped inside
the human heart;
it is the gift of love.

Marie T. Freeman

*I*f we love one another, God abides in us,

and His love is perfected in us.

1 John 4:12 NASB

A friend loves at all times.

Proverbs 17:17 NIV

Since love grows within you, so beauty grows.
                For love is the beauty of the soul.

Saint Augustine

See that ye love one another with a pure heart fervently.

1 Peter 1:22 KJV

The whole being of any Christian is faith and love.

Faith brings the man to God;

love brings him to men.

Martin Luther

Give me such love for God and men as will blot out
all hatred and bitterness.

Dietrich Bonhoeffer

Only joyous love redeems.

Catherine Marshall

Carve your name on hearts, not on marble.

C. H. Spurgeon

A Christmas Prayer

*Lord, during this season when we celebrate the birth of Your Son,
help me to show kindness to all those who cross my path, and
let me show tenderness and unfailing love to my family and friends.
Make me generous with words of encouragement and praise.
And, help me always to reflect the love that Christ Jesus
gave me so that through me, others might find Him.*

Amen

GOD'S GRACE

For by grace are ye saved through faith; and that not of yourselves:
it is the gift of God: not of works, lest any man should boast.

Ephesians 2:8-9 KJV

On the very first Christmas day, when God sent His Son to become the salvation of the world, He bestowed a gift that is beyond price and beyond human comprehension. We have not earned our salvation; even the best among us fall far short of God's commandments. But, when we accept Christ as our savior, we are saved by God's grace. Let us praise God for His gift, and let us share His Good News with the world.

*C*ostly grace is the treasure hidden in the field;

for the sake of it, a man will gladly go

and sell all that he has. It is costly because

it costs a man his life, and it is grace because it gives

a man the only true life.

Dietrich Bonhoeffer

The life of faith is a daily exploration of the constant and
countless ways in which God's grace and
love are experienced.

Eugene Peterson

The grace of God is infinite and eternal. As it had no beginning,
so it can have no end, and being an attribute of God,
it is as boundless as infinitude.

A. W. Tozer

GOD'S GRACE

*G*race is not about finishing last or first;

it is about not counting.

We receive grace as a gift from God,

not as something we toil to earn.

Philip Yancey

But Jesus immediately said to them:

"Take courage!

It is I. Don't be afraid."

Matthew 14:27 NIV

*T*he Christmas story gives its triumphant answer:

"Be not afraid."

Karl Barth

A Christmas Prayer

*Dear Lord, during the Christmas season and throughout the year,
I praise You for Your priceless gifts. You have saved me by Your grace.
Keep me mindful that Your grace is a gift that I can accept but cannot earn.
Let me share the good news of Your grace with a world that
desperately needs Your healing touch.*

Amen

A TIME FOR PRAYER

Watch ye therefore, and pray always . . . .

Luke 21:36 KJV

The Christmas season is a time when we offer thanks for Jesus and for the One who sent Him. We express thanksgiving through our words, through our deeds, and through our prayers.

Jesus instructed His followers to pray always, and His advice applies to Christians of every generation. When we weave the habit of prayer into the very fabric of our days, we invite God to become a partner in every aspect of our lives. And, when we make the Christmas season a time of thanksgiving and prayer, we welcome the Christ child into our hearts, which, of course, is exactly where He belongs.

*W*hether we think of, or speak to, God,

whether we act or suffer for Him,

all is prayer when we have no other object than

His love and the desire of pleasing Him.

John Wesley

If I should neglect prayer but a single day,
I should lose a great deal of the fire of faith.

Martin Luther

Don't pray when you feel like it; make an appointment
with the King and keep it.

Corrie ten Boom

Get into the habit of dealing with God about everything.

Oswald Chambers

If the spiritual life is to be healthy and under the full power of
the Holy Spirit, praying without ceasing will be natural.

Andrew Murray

Wasted time of which we are later ashamed, temptations we yield to,
weaknesses, lethargy in our work, disorder and lack of discipline
in our thoughts and in our interaction with others—all these
frequently have their root in neglecting prayer in the morning.

Dietrich Bonhoeffer

He who kneels most stands best.

D. L. Moody

The effective prayer of a righteous man
can accomplish much.

James 5:16 NASB

*A*sk and it shall be given to you; seek and you shall find;

knock and it shall be opened to you.

For every one who asks receives, and he who seeks finds . . . .

Matthew 7:7-8 NASB

A Christmas Prayer

Lord, as I celebrate the birth of Jesus, keep me mindful that Christmas is a time for thanksgiving and prayer. I pray to You, Father, because You desire it and because I need it. Prayer not only changes things; it also changes me. Make me a prayerful Christian, Lord, and let me turn every aspect of my life over to You, today and forever.

Amen

PEACE ON EARTH

These things I have spoken unto you, that in me ye might have peace.

John 16:33 KJV

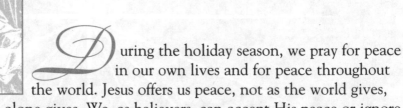

During the holiday season, we pray for peace in our own lives and for peace throughout the world. Jesus offers us peace, not as the world gives, but as He alone gives. We, as believers, can accept His peace or ignore it. When we accept the peace of Jesus Christ into our hearts, our lives are transformed and the promise of the Christmas season is fulfilled.

Peace with God is where all peace begins.

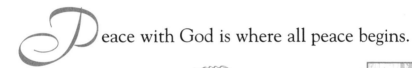

Jim Gallery

And suddenly there was with the angel a multitude of the heavenly host praising God, and saying,

Glory to God in the highest, and on earth peace,

good will toward men.

Luke 2:13-14 NASB

He brought peace on earth and wants to bring it also into your soul,
that peace which the world cannot give.

Corrie ten Boom

The Christmas message is that there is hope for humanity,
hope of pardon, hope of peace with God, hope of glory.

J. I. Packer

Look around you and you'll be distressed; look within yourself
and you'll be depressed; look at Jesus,
and you'll be at rest!

Corrie ten Boom

*S*ilent Night! Holy Night!

All is calm, all is bright.

Round yon virgin mother and child!

Holy infant so tender and mild,

Sleep in heavenly peace, sleep in heavenly peace.

Father Joseph Mohr, 1818

I heard the bells on Christmas Day,
Their old familiar carols play,
And wild and sweet their words repeat
Of peace on earth, good-will to men!

Henry Wadsworth Longfellow

*A*s fits the holy Christmas birth,

Be this, good friends, our carol still

Be peace on earth, be peace on earth,

To men of gentle will.

William Makepeace Thackeray

It Came Upon a Midnight Clear

It came upon the midnight clear,

that glorious song of old,

From angels bending near the earth,

to touch their harps of gold.

*P*eace on the earth, goodwill to men,

from heav'n's all gracious king,

The world in solemn stillness lay to hear the angels sing.

Edmund Sears, 1850

A Christmas Prayer

Lord, when I turn my thoughts and my prayers to Jesus,
I am blessed. On these days when I celebrate Christ's birth,
let me welcome Him into my heart, and let me accept His peace,
not just for today, but for all eternity.

Amen

A TIME FOR WORSHIP AND PRAISE

Is anyone happy? Let him sing songs of praise.

James 5:13 NIV

*N*othing should obscure the fact that Christmas is the annual birthday celebration of the Christian faith. Christmas day is, first and forever, a religious holiday—a time for Christians everywhere to rejoice, to pray, and to worship God. During this holiday season, it is proper that we keep our eyes, our voices, and our hearts lifted upward as we offer profound thanksgiving to God through our worship and through our praise.

Praise Him! Praise Him!

Tell of His excellent greatness;

Praise Him! Praise Him!

Ever in joyful song.

Fanny Crosby

O Come All Ye Faithful

O come all ye faithful, joyful and triumphant,

O come ye, O come ye to Bethlehem

Come and behold him, born the King of angels,

O come let us adore him,

O come let us adore him,

O come let us adore him,

Christ the Lord.

Sing, choirs of angels, sing in exultation,

Sing all ye citizens of heaven above,

Glory to God, all glory in the highest,

O come let us adore him,

O come let us adore him,

O come let us adore him,

Christ the Lord.

Latin Carol, 18th Century

Make a joyful noise unto the Lord all ye lands.

Serve the Lord with gladness:

come before his presence with singing.

Know ye that the Lord he is God:

it is he that hath made us, and not we ourselves;

we are his people and the sheep of his pasture.

Enter into his gates with thanksgiving,

and into his courts with praise;

be thankful unto him and bless his name.

For the Lord is good; his mercy is everlasting;

and his truth endureth to all generations.

Psalm 100, KJV

Our God is the sovereign Creator of the universe!
He loves us as His own children and has provided
every good thing we have; He is worthy
of our praise every moment.

Shirley Dobson

To praise God is to please God.

Jim Gallery

Praise—lifting up our heart and hands, exulting with our voices,
singing his praises—is the occupation of those
who dwell in the kingdom.

Max Lucado

I will praise the name of God with a song,

and will magnify him

with thanksgiving.

Psalm 69:30 KJV

J was glad when they said unto me,

Let us go

into the house of the LORD.

Psalm 122:1 KJV

*W*orship is not taught from the pulpit.
It must be learned in the heart.

Jim Elliot

A Christmas Prayer

Lord, let Christmas day and every day be a time of worship.
Whether I am in Your house or simply going about
my daily activities, let me worship You, not only with words
and deeds, but also with my heart. In my quiet moments,
let me praise You and thank You for creating me,
for loving me, for guiding me,
and for saving me.

Amen

JOY TO THE WORLD

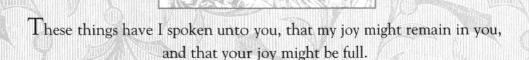

These things have I spoken unto you, that my joy might remain in you,
and that your joy might be full.

John 15:11 KJV

Christ made it clear to His followers: He intended that His joy would become their joy. And it still holds true today: Christ intends that His believers share His love with His joy in their hearts. This Christmas season let us accept the joy that is ours through the One who gave His life so that we might have life abundant and eternal.

If you who have a troubled heart,

listen to the angel's song:

"I bring you tiding of great joy!"

Jesus did not come to condemn you.

If you want to define Christ rightly,

then pay heed to how the angel defines Him:

"A great joy!"

Martin Luther

Joy is the serious business of heaven.

C. S. Lewis

When God blesses us, He expects us to use those blessings
to bless the lives of others.

Jim Gallery

The manger is a symbol of what can happen
when Jesus Christ resides in us.

Bill Hybels

*M*ay the God of hope fill you with all joy and

peace as you trust in him,

so that you may overflow with hope by the power

of the Holy Spirit.

Romans 15:13 NIV

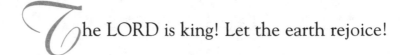

he LORD is king! Let the earth rejoice!

Psalm 97:1 NLT

What is your focus today? Joy comes when it is Jesus first, others second . . . then you.

Kay Arthur

Gratitude changes the pangs of memory into a tranquil joy.

Dietrich Bonhoeffer

Joy to the World

Joy to the world! The Lord is come!

Let earth receive her king.

Let every heart prepare Him room,

and heaven and nature sing,

and heaven and nature sing, and heaven,

and heaven, and nature sing.

Isaac Watts, 1719

*L*et the hearts of those who seek the Lord rejoice.

Look to the Lord and his strength;

seek his face always.

1 Chronicles 16:10-11 NIV

*W*hen Jesus Christ is the source of our joy, no words can describe it.

Billy Graham

149

God Rest You Merry Gentlemen

God rest you merry, gentlemen,

Let nothing you dismay,

Remember Christ our Savior

Was born on Christmas Day,

To save us all from Satan's pow'r

When we were gone astray;

O tidings of comfort and joy,

comfort and joy,

O tidings of comfort and joy.

18th Century English Carol

Rejoicing is clearly a spiritual command. To ignore it,
I need to remind you, is disobedience.

C. H. Spurgeon

Rejoice, the Lord is King; Your Lord and King adore!
Rejoice, give thanks and sing and triumph evermore.

Charles Wesley

There is not one blade of grass, there is no color in this world
that is not intended to make us rejoice.

John Calvin

*C*hristmas means the beginning of Christianity and a second chance for the world.

Peter Marshall

A Christmas Prayer

Lord, make me a joyous Christian. Because of my salvation through Your Son, I have every reason to celebrate life. During this Christmas season, let me share the joyful news of Jesus Christ, and let my life be a testimony to His love and to His grace.

Amen

REFERENCES

Scripture taken from the HOLY BIBLE, NEW INTERNATIONAL VERSION ©. NIV ©. Copyright © 1973, 1978, 1984, by International Bible Society. Used by permission of Zondervan Publishing House. All rights reserved.

Scripture taken from the New American Standard Bible®, Copyright © 1960, 1962, 1963, 1968, 1971, 1972, 1973, 1975, 1977, 1995 by The Lockman Foundation. Used by permission.

Scripture quotations marked (NLT) are taken from The Holy Bible, New Living Translation, Copyright © 1996. Used by permission of Tyndale House Publishers, Incorporated, Wheaton, Illinois 60189. All rights reserved.